Living by Faith

A Journey of Love & Encouragement

Mary E. Darby

All poems are written by Mary E. Darby

Edited by: Sylvia White-Irby, Nicole White-Gamble and Leslye Kasoff

Cover Design by: Juan Roberts, Creative Lunacy
CreativeLunacy1.blogspot.com

Library of Congress Control Number: 2012936313

ISBN: 978-0-9854107-0-4

For information regarding permission or additional copies, contact the publisher:

KNOWLEDGE POWER BOOKS
A Division of Knowledge Power Communications, Inc.
25379 Wayne Mills Place, Suite 131
Valencia, CA 91355
www.knowledgepowerbooks.com

Printed in the United States

Living by Faith

is a special gift for:

_____

From:

_____

Date:

_____

Living by Faith

A Journey of Love & Encouragement

Mary E. Darby

A Collection of Poetry

Table of Contents

Dedication
Acknowledgement
Preface

Dedication

I dedicate *Living by Faith* to my beloved mother, Ann Richardson, affectionately known as "Big Ma" and my dear grandson Brandon Gamble.

"I can do all things through Christ
which strengthens me."

Philippians 4:13

Acknowledgements

To God, my heavenly Father, who has given me the gifts that I am able to share with you. To God be all the glory.

I thank all of the people who helped make this dream a reality—my dear daughters Nicole and Sylvia, who gave love and support, and a host of others who supported and encouraged me to pursue my goal. Many thanks to those who have read my poems over the years and provided suggestions that inspired my creativity. They were with me every step of the way.

I would also like to thank the Spirit and Life Ministries family, especially Pastor Hamilton, Carla and Minister Payne. The prayers and blessings from my church family continue to inspire and lift me up.

My dedicated family, including son-in-law Edward, Ernest; loving sisters Gail, Richardine, Ann, Theresa, Loretta, Ruby; favorite nephews Darryl and Ronnie; Sahran, who is a joy; Aunt Barbara and my many loving nieces, nephews and cousins; the Gamble family; and goddaughters LaTanya, Lillian, Evette, Barbara, Leslye, Chrystal, Monica, Susan and Latricia. Caring neighbors the Kellers, Clin and Lanette and Joan and Bob. Loving and supportive friends Linda, Diane, Essie, Doris, Angela, Howard and Beverly; and childhood friends Claudine and Yvonne.

My heartfelt thanks to the loving nurses and staff of the Neurosurgery Unit (NSU), including Marissa, Valentino, Sara, Dr. Harsimran Brara, Nam, Peter and Richard.   A special thanks to the nurses and staff in the Intensive Care and Cardiac units. Immeasurable appreciation to the Glendale Adventist Rehabilitation physical therapy team and nurses, especially Dr. Aaron Selzer, Martin, Robin, Julius, Paul, Rihanna, Art and Jenna. I am forever grateful for the support of Dr. Arya Saleh, Dr. John Gamble II and Dr. Brian Gamble.

Special thanks to Willa Robinson, who encouraged me to publish my poems and patiently worked with me to make this possible. My life has truly been a miracle, and I will continue to Live by Faith.

Preface

Living by Faith is a collection of poems inspired by the many experiences that have drawn me closer to God. I began writing when I was a young girl, as a way to quietly express my inner thoughts. I have always enjoyed conveying my life lessons through poetry. I hope my journey can inspire the inner spirit that lives within all of us.

By Faith

"Trust in the LORD with all your heart and lean not on your own understanding; in all your ways acknowledge him, and he will make your paths straight."
Proverbs 3:5-6

I'm Going to Catch on to Jesus' Hand

I'm going to catch on to Jesus' hand,
Tell that old devil I'm going to stand.

I'm going to fight with all my might,
I know with Jesus everything is going to be alright.

I'm going to shout and tell the story,
How My Lord has brought me glory.

It's going to be a brand new day,
I'm going to let the Lord have His way.

I'm going to sing and I will shout,
Thank God, He has brought me out.

He brought me from the lion's den,
He fought my battles so I could win.

I can hear my Master say,
Come unto me child today.

I'm going to lean on my Jesus' arm,
I know He will protect me from all harm.

I'm going to give Jesus my heart,
I know He will give me a brand new start.

I'm going to put on my shinny shield,
I'm going to do my God's will.

I Am Fighting For My Life

I have a battle I don't want to lose,
God gave me the power to choose.

I am fighting for my life,
Jesus has already paid the price.

Paul said never stop striving,
Jesus is the key for surviving.

There is evil I see but I'm blind,
I gave Jesus my soul and mind.

There is a war going on,
I must block the devil all day long.

I need Jesus to direct my ways,
He alone can lengthen my days.

I must never give up this fight,
I pray to God to give me might.

I surrender my all to God,
He is my shield, sword, and heart.

I ran to Him and he was there,
I accept His love and know He cares.

My faith in Him will not let me die,
My victory comes from up high.

Living by Faith

Do I live by law and just follow the rules?

I can stand on the mountain top,
And have a dream like Martin Luther King.

I can strive to help mankind,
Like Gandhi, I can do remarkable things.

I can discern what is honest,
I will have power to choose right.

I can surrender my will to Jesus,
Like the blind gaining sight.

I can wake up rejoicing,
Because He wakes me up.

I can forgive my enemies,
I will refuse to be corrupt.

I can sense His holy presence,
I believe He makes me whole.

I can fly like the birds,
I have joy in my soul.

I can stop judging my brother,
I will correct my own evil ways.

I can listen to what God is saying,
Put my trust in Him always.

I can accept my state the good or bad,
I can sing about His amazing grace.

I can kneel before the King,
And be thankful for His goodness.

I can believe in His love everlasting.
And know that I have been blessed.

Mary E. Darby

I Choose to Live

Living is the desire to live

Feeling the spirit inside

Facing trials and tribulations

Striving to keep my soul

Clinging to Jesus for life

Keeping my faith

Choosing to love my brother

Removing all fears and doubts

Hearing the Word of God

Following Jesus' directions

Speaking kind words

Choosing to walk in the Light

Choosing to live for Jesus

Choosing to live

Faith

I saw a bird flying free,
Then, I realized that it was me.

I felt the cool summer breeze,
Suddenly, my spirit felt at ease.

I smelled the fragrance of a flower,
Peace cleansed me like a shower.

I tasted the honey of a honeycomb,
I learned to forgive and to move on.

I dreamed of God's amazing grace,
I knew, I must strive and keep my faith.

Faith is Dancing on a Cloud

I am
Dancing on a cloud,
I am singing out loud.

I am
Glad to be me,
I am thankful to be free.

I see
Beauty all around,
My purpose I have found.

I am
Relaxed like a dove,
My help comes from above.

I am
Whole and bold,
My presence has unfolded.

I am
Here and now,
I have God to show me how.

I am
A shining star,
My faith will take me far.

Life is a Gift

I'm having the time of my life,
No time for malice, hatred or strife.

It took years for me to accept being free,
I visualize myself climbing to the top of a big oak tree.

My past holds memories but my present holds now,
Each day I will find the joy of living, I vow.

The miracle lives within my soul,
There to empower and make me bold.

I feel the love of forgiving,
I have learned the worth of living.

I make the choice of how I live,
I make the choice to take or give.

I blame no one for my mistakes,
Being responsible is all it takes.

I change my thoughts and change my mind,
It helps me discover what I want to find.

My worth is no more or less than others,
I believe in my heart that we all are brothers.

The things I own are just a loan,
What can I take with me when I am gone?

I pray that my life has helped someone,
I pray that my Maker will say, well done.

At That Moment

At that moment,
I felt His presence,
I knew His power.

At that moment,
I could hear the angels,
Singing of His glory forever more.

At that moment,
I accepted His Word,
I had found the key.

At that moment,
My eyes were wide open,
Jesus set me free.

I Cherish This Moment

This very moment, instance, second,
I feel great and at peace with myself.
Everything I ever wanted or needed I possess,
Everything I need exists inside of me.
I feel the love for me.
The me I was, the me I am and the me to be,
I see a free spirit allowing me to dance in open space
Free without fear of what others will think.
I can love because I have love for myself
Love to give to someone else.
I have joy knowing I was created for a purpose,
A sense of life, peace and happiness
I did not earn it or do anything to deserve it
Everything that I have that is worthwhile
is absolutely free
God created me for a purpose,
He wants me to have life and to have
it more abundantly.
He has given me talents to use to help
myself and others.
God knows my every move from beginning to end.
He loves me unconditionally.
He offers me eternal life.
He teaches me the elements of true love.
He teaches me how to love my brothers and sisters.
Jesus Christ is my Savior.
I fear no man
I face no problem that I cannot overcome through
Jesus Christ, My Savior

I Can Depend on God

I can always put my trust in God,
There is not anything that is too hard.

I know when I seek Him, He will be there,
I know His judgment is righteous and fair.

He gave me everything that I need,
With His guidance I will succeed.

No greater peace will I ever find,
He is in my heart and calms my mind.

He loves me in spite of my mistakes,
I know it is His will if I awake.

God's love fills me up and keeps me high,
It gives me hope and that is why.

There is no mystery about what He can do,
He is God Almighty and He loves you too.

There is nothing too hard for my God,
He looks at me and He sees my heart.

He picks me up when I let myself down,
He dries my tears and smoothes away my frown.

He gives me serenity that I had not known,
He gives me a clear mind that I can call my own.

He opened my eyes and opened up the view,
God made my sick body feel brand new.

When I felt that my time was very near,
I felt His presence and I had no fear.

It is unspeakable joy that my God brings,
My God is all power and can do all things.

My Faith Remains

My faith remains steadfast,
I don't worry how long my troubles will last.

I have inner peace from deep within,
My joy lasts from the beginning to the end.

I have let go of problems and depend on the Lord,
My life has become simple rather than hard.

I welcome my presence, the here and now,
My spirit has awaken and shown me how.

I have forgiven even my worst enemy,
It gave me freedom and set me free.

I am able to love with a clean heart,
My love for my brother keeps me closer to God.

I value people much more than I do things,
My life has meaning and the joy it brings.

When I am still and feel my spirit divine,
My body is calm and I have peace of mind.

I have stopped blaming and judging others,
Now I can see myself in my brothers.

My soul sings victory and knows it will win,
I laid down my burdens and let Jesus in.

My God is My Safe Place

My God is my safe place,

He walks with me wherever I go.

When I am slipping and sliding,

In the fluffy white snow.

My God is my safe place,

While I run and play outside.

Chasing after my good friends,

To catch them before they hide.

My God is my safe place,

Like a soft blanket to keep me warm.

I keep Him close to my heart,

He protects me from harm.

I Know He Loves Me

When I am all alone,
My God is there on His throne,
And I know He loves me.

Many people have passed me by,
Have made me want to weep and cry,
But I know He loves me.

Troubles come and troubles go,
This one thing I surely know,
I know He loves me.

Sometimes when I am feeling down,
Jesus lifts me up from the ground,
I know He loves me.

There is no way to be free,
Without my God leading me,
I know He loves me.

He tells me how I can live,
He gives me more than I can give,
I know He loves me.

There is no other one that I know,
That is there for me wherever I go,
I know He loves me.

He hears me whenever I pray,
He listens to what I have to say,
I know He loves me.

He has taken away all my fears,
His name is sweet music to my ears,
I know He loves me.

He is there morning, noon and night,
He tells me everything is going to be all right,
I know He loves me.

I have nothing to boast about,
But this one thing I will shout,
I know He loves me.

I Have Seen a Miracle

I have seen a miracle in me,
God rescued my soul and set it free.
I have seen a miracle in me,
I am not the same person I use to be.

I was dying with each passing day,
God stirred my heart and paved my way.
My life was filled with so much pain,
God touched my body and restored it again.

I have seen a miracle in me,
God changed my failure to possibilities.
I was wandering like a lost soul,
God restored my life and made me whole.

I have fallen down so low,
God lifted me and told me where to go.
There were times I was too weak to talk,
God taught me how to stand and walk.

I have seen a miracle in me,
God has given me liberty.
I had a broken mind and heart,
God has given me a brand new start.

I seen a miracle in me,
God has guaranteed victory.
I was alone without a friend,
God promised to be with me to the end.

I have seen a miracle I can soar,
I know that God's love is forever more.
I have seen a miracle save this sinner,
My God has made me a winner.

You Gave Me Everything

You gave me life,
I can choose to live forever.

You gave me joy,
Deep down within my soul.

You gave me hope,
I do not have to worry about tomorrow.

You gave me peace,
Calm as a brook with clear water.

You gave me love,
Unconditional and available for me.

You gave me faith,
To conquer life's turbulent storms.

You gave me a choice,
I can choose to be evil or good.

You gave me the will to survive,
The devil flees from where you dwell.

God is Watching You

Sometimes you may ask, what would Jesus do?
Remember that God is always watching you.

He knows how you think and knows what you mean,
He knows your hopes and all of your dreams.

He sees your inside as well as the out,
He knows your ways and what you're all about.

He sees everything that you do,
He hears every word and He knows what is true.

He sees your good deeds and your bad,
He knows what you got and what you've had.

There is nothing from God that you can conceal,
God made you and knows just how you feel.

He sees you rise in the morning and lie down at night,
He knows when you're wrong and when you're right.

He sees you struggling with evil and sin,
He watches and waits to be invited to come in.

He sees your strengths and your weakness clear,
He sees the things you value and you hold dear.

He sees beyond your titles or worldly possessions,
He sees where your heart is and hears your confessions.

He sees what you do, it outweighs what you say,
He sees what you need before you bow to pray.

He sees when you stumble or when you fall down,
He sees if you will get up or remain on the ground.

He sees you using His Holy name in vain,
He sees you using His Holy name for personal gain.

He sees you fighting and killing one another,
He sees you hating and mistreating your brother.

God sees the real you without the mask,
He sees where you are going and He knows your past.

He sees your suffering and He sees your pain,
He sees your faith because you know He is coming again.

So remember that God is always watching you,
And decide to do what Jesus would do.

There is No Job Too Big for God

You constantly worry about everything,
Trying to fix your entire problems yourself.

You feel downhearted because nothing seems right,
The mountain looks too hard for you to climb.

You think about the confusion in the world,
How can you make it through the day?

People fall short of being trustworthy,
Friends are not always there.

Loved ones slip away and leave memories,
Your heart weeps when you are alone.

Do not worry about your tomorrows,
God has you in His plan.

There is no problem too big for Him to handle,
He is just a prayer away.

Lean on Him with all of your strength,
He will support your every need.

Cry out to Him from your deepest sorrow,
Know that He will fix your broken heart.

He loves you more than anyone loves you,
He is your Father and knows what you can bear.

There is no friend like Jesus,
He will pluck you from a burning furnace.

He carries you through storms you have not seen,
He suffered so that you could live more abundantly.

He sends angels to come and encourage you,
Ignore the devil trying to steal your blessings.

There is no problem too big for God,
You are His child He created in His own image.

Move mountains by calling on His name,
You have power because you have God.

Tell Him all about your troubles,
He waits for your invitation to be saved.

There is no problem too big for God,
Your creator knows what you need.

Imagine

Imagine the Father's love,
For His only begotten son.

Imagine taking His life,
In order to save everyone.

Imagine the pain He feels,
When we sin and let Him down.

Imagine His faithfulness,
Eternally being around.

Imagine being as small as sand,
Always in the Master's view.

Imagine how you treat someone,
Will eventually come back to you.

Imagine you have this moment,
Cherish it as if it were your last.

Imagine God has control,
Over your future and your past.

Imagine

What is Life About

It is not where you have been,
It is about where you are going.

It is not about who you know,
It is about what you know.

It is not about how long you live,
It is about how you live.

It is not about knowing what is right,
It is about doing what is right.

It is not about caring for things,
It is about caring for people.

It is not about what a person says,
It is about what a person does.

It is not about judging others' actions,
It is about judging your own actions.

It is not about how much you know,
It is about how you use what you know.

It is not about who loves, you,
It is about you loving yourself.

It is not about taking vengeance.
It is about having mercy.

It is not about how many friends you have,
It is about how many are your friend.

It is not about what others think about you,
It is about what you think about yourself.

It is not about living for tomorrow,
It is about living in the present.

That Inner Feeling

It is mine only to touch,
I feel like a bird soaring in the sky,
I joyfully shout to the gospel.

It is inside me filling my heart with glee,
Deep within the soul my spirit tingles,
Assuring me that all is well.

Like the sun rising to light the earth,
I bloom into Spring like a new birth,
Richer than a king and free.

Standing high looking over the valley,
Knowing that I can make a safe landing,
I am in touch with my Maker.

Hearing the sounds of angels singing,
Awakening God's creation in the heart,
Capturing endless love.

Peace embraces my inner thoughts,
Like waterfalls flowing over rocks,
Polishing all of the rough edges.

Its birth is like a mustard seed,
Growing and spreading within me,
Giving me a life line to climb.

Body, mind, and heart becomes one,
Focusing on the Lord,
Surrendering all to Him.

Having a reason for living,
Experiencing I am not alone,
Accepting the power of God.

Everything We Need to Succeed

We can decide to be happy or sad,
One feels good and the other feels bad.

We can be delighted to be who we are,
In our own eyes become a superstar.

When we hear the sound of our favorite song,
Imagine things that went right rather than wrong.

We can begin at any time day or night,
It is never too late to get it right.

We can start the day looking for the sun to shine,
If we look for the good, that is what we will find.

Decide what we want out of life and then claim it,
Do we want abundance or just a little bit.

Love, Peace, Happiness, Hope and Faith awaits us,
Ask for what we want and it will come true.

We have a purpose in life that hungers to be fed,
We must put positive thoughts in our heads.

We must find something that makes us laugh,
That will direct our feelings to a joyful path.

We can travel with someone going our way,
But if they are not we should not stay.

We can work for peace instead of war,
We can make love the cause we strive for.

Who Is He?

Again Jesus spoke to them, saying, "I am the light of the world. Whoever follows me will never walk in darkness but will have the light of life."
John 8:12

Holy Spirit

He came to me while I was yet a child,
He entered my sick room and stayed awhile.

He talked to me and calmed my fears,
He comforted me and wiped away my tears.

He let me know that I was not alone,
He told me that I was His own.

He shined the sunlight for me to see,
He sent the robins to sing to me.

He healed my body and saved my soul,
He brought me peace and made me whole.

He made fluffy white clouds up in the sky,
He let me watch them as they floated by.

He shook the green leaves in the trees,
He created a nice cool summer breeze.

He listened to me and answered my requests,
He never failed to give me the best,

He gave me hope and the will to live,
He inspired the testimony I have to give.

He delivered me while I was yet a child,
He entered my sick room and stayed awhile.

He Alone

If you want to change someone else,
You need to start working on yourself.

You will have to answer to God,
He is the one to judge your heart.

He alone can wash away your sins,
He is your Maker and your friend.

Do not put your faith in man,
Put your faith in God's hands.

Trust in Him and Him alone,
He will be there when others are gone.

Troubles will come and sometimes go,
Wait on the Lord, this you should know.

The One

If knowledge is power,
Then I've found the key.

I have found the one,
Who truly loves me.

I've searched for meaning,
Asking why do I live.

He has the answer,
He is willing to give.

I took a moment,
I looked all around.

Once I was lost,
But now I am found.

Through all of my suffering,
My tears and my pain.

He brings me hope,
I will smile again.

How precious His gift,
It directs my path.

God touches my heart,
And my spirit laughs.

Life Begins and Ends with Jesus

When I need a friend, He befriends me.
When I am lonely, He comforts me.
When I am depressed, He gives me joy.
When I am sick, He heals me.
When I seek knowledge, He gives me the Bible.
When I am weak, He renews my strength.
When I need love, He loves me.
When I am confused, He gives me understanding.
When I need hope, He makes all things possible.
When I am lost, He directs me
to the path of righteousness.
When I need protection, He builds
a hedge all around me.
When I need peace, He gives me peace.
When I am hungry, He feeds me.
When I face death, He offers eternal life.
When I am weary, He lifts me up.
When I face my enemies, He fights my battles.
When I am blind, He gives me sight.
When I am drowning in despair, Jesus is my Savior.

My God

My God is a mighty God.
He strengthens me.
He strengthens you.
He strengthens us.

My God is a loving God.
He loves me.
He loves you.
He loves us.

My God is an all knowing God.
He knows me.
He knows you.
He knows us.

My God is a merciful God.
He has mercy for me.
He has mercy for you.
He has mercy for us.

My God is the Creator.
He created me.
He created you.
He created us.

My God listens to my prayers.
He hears me.
He hears you.
He hears us.

My God is righteous.
He is good to me.
He is good to you.
He is good to us.

What Matters

I can diet and be thin as a dime,

I can clean my house until it shines.

I can get many degrees and learn many things,

I can earn all kinds of titles and be a king.

I can buy everything I want to own,

I can be very popular and never alone.

I can appear to the world to have it all,

But without Jesus Christ I will surely fall.

All I Ever Wanted

All I ever wanted was to be happy,
Just to find my peace of mind.
I wanted to be loved,
To be accepted by someone divine.

I hoped to be needed,
To be a part of something greater than me.
I dreamed of freedom,
That would set my soul free.

I asked for forgiveness,
I strived to mend my ways.
I wanted deliverance,
To serve the Lord all my days.

I wanted to be satisfied,
To be content in God's Word.
All I ever wanted was to give praise,
And to let my thanks be heard.

What I Could Not Do For Myself

God knew me before I was born,
He gave me strength to carry on.
He knew me before I knew myself.

He loves unconditionally,
It was His love that set me free,
He loved when I didn't love myself.

God has helped me through the tough years,
He knows just how to calm my fears,
He helped when I couldn't help myself.

He is my Master and my friend,
God blessed my soul with peace within,
I could not find peace for myself.

God cleaned me up and made me whole,
He gave me life finer than gold,
He cleaned what I couldn't cleanse myself.

God saved me and gave me grace,
He leadth me to win this race,
He saved me from my wicked self.

He brought me joy and goodness too,
There isn't anything that God can't do,
He brought what I couldn't give myself.

He offered me life forever more,
Shackled the devil and locked the door,
He's the Way, I am lost without Him.

God taught me real humility,
How serving others sets me free,
He taught how to humble myself.

God paid the price that I might live,
He's faithful, my sins He forgives,
I am penniless by myself.

You Did Not Have to Save Me

You did not have to give me life, but you did.
You did not have to love me, but you did

You did not have to provide for me, but you did.
You did not have to set me free, but you did.

You did not have to pick me up, but you did.
You did not have to stand by me, but you did.

You did not have to protect me, but you did.
You did not have to touch my heart, but you did.

You did not have to save my life, but you did.
You did not have to die for me, but you did.

The Refreshing Air of God

Oh, how refreshing to breathe God's clean air,
And to know that He has given me another day.

Everything that should be has happened for a purpose,
I am a part of God's plan because He has blessed me.

My heart beats with joy that I have life right now,
I have no worry for tomorrow that is not promised.

This is the time for me to sing and praise His name,
How good it is to know the love of God and hope.

With His Holy Spirit to guide me I have no fear,
I can soar to the highest mountain and not tire.

It is God's grace that gives me the freedom to live,
I am glad I let go and allowed God to save my soul.

I awaken to a new birth that is my choice,
My mind is clear and calm with gratefulness.

I am able to forgive as I have been forgiven,
All I have belongs to my Lord and Savior.

Oh, what joy and peace that heals all my ailments,
I am not worthy but God made me complete.

Hope

The joy
Of loving God,
It is complete fulfillment.

The peace
In knowing God,
Calms your soul and gives rest.

The faith
Of believing in God,
Gives hope to survive each day.

The power
Of depending on God,
Strengthens your heart and soul.

Revealed

It's so plain and clear and easy,
No muddy water to blur the images,
No false illusions of perfection,
No grand disillusions of accomplishments,
No mistaken identity,
No false pride to be displayed.

Replacements of a higher order,
Hope filled with sunshine,
Peace that embraces well being,
A handle on life,
Love for God's creations,
Witnessing a miracle,
Faith in Jesus' return,
Accepting Jesus in my heart and soul.

I Am Full

I am full Lord,
I am filled by your grace.

I am full Lord,
I find peace in this place.

I am full Lord,
My soul feels your love.

I am full Lord,
I believe there's a heaven above.

I am full Lord,
I cast out my pain and sorrow.

I am full Lord,
I no longer worry about tomorrow.

I am full Lord,
I sing praises to you each day.

I am full Lord,
I thank you for showing me the way.

I Am Loved

I am loved,
He is more than the love of my life.

I know deep down within,
His love gives me life.

I wake up with Thanksgiving,
I know, He is near me.

Wherever I go, I take Him with me,
Surely I have done nothing to deserve His love.

I look forward to every moment,
My love tells me not to worry about anything.

I have courage to do the best that I can,
I know He is a problem solver.

I am weak but my love gives me strength,
When I stumble, He directs my path.

My attitude has become grateful and positive,
Oh, how wonderful it is to have such a love.

He gives me wings to fly like an eagle,
My love brings hope and faith to my soul.

I can do all things for good because of Him,
Without my love I am like unmolded clay.

He teaches me how to be patient,
My faith and hope is stored in my heart.

He restores my vision that I might see,
The greatest gift I have is His love.

I Found the Perfect Love

Time had no meaning,
I walked with the blind.

I kept right on searching,
Looking for peace of mind.

Things all around me,
I found no happiness.

My friends tried to help,
But I cared less.

I heard a voice,
It came from deep inside.

It said let go,
Release your ego and pride.

What you seek you have,
It is love.

I fell to my knees,
I prayed to God above.

Suddenly, I felt it,
It moved from head to toe.

Giving me comfort,
I longed to know.

I found the perfect love,
That gives me life.

Sweet joy I've never known,
No more sorrow or strife.

My Friend and Savior

Thank you dear Lord for loving me,
Though I have not done anything to deserve it.
You comfort me when I am lonely,
I know that you are there for me.

You soothe away my heartache and pain,
You bring joy into my soul.
You touch my heart and awaken it to love,
Love for my fellow man and my enemies.

You have taught me the meaning of forgiveness,
I can forgive others and myself.
Just to have your guiding light,
Renews my strength and my faith.

I know one thing with certainty,
You are my Lord and Savior.
I will put my soul in your hands for safety,
I will serve thee all the days of my life.

I have learned that my imperfections,
Will be corrected by God's perfection.
Your wisdom is beyond my understanding,
Thank you for giving me life.

None Other

There is no joy like knowing the Lord,
There is no peace that I can find.

There is no love that reaches the soul,
Like the divine love of our Father.

There is no treasure that one can possess,
Like the wealth that He gives to enrich.

There is no comfort like His strength,
Holding me up from life's dilemmas.

There is no other protection,
Like the shield of the almighty God.

There is no knowledge without Him,
He reveals wisdom to stay alive.

There is no other supreme being,
Like my God that is all powerful.

My God and Your God the Same

My God and Your God are the same,
He knows us all by our first names.

We are all equal in His eyes,
Our needs He can satisfy.

He loves us in spite of our sins,
He welcomes us all to come in.

My brothers come take my hand,
Let's travel to the Promise Land.

We can call His direct line,
He's available all of the time.

He has built us a special place,
Come let us run this old race.

He sees our heart and knows our beat,
He makes our empty lives complete.

He is not impressed by our feats,
Death was His victory to defeat.

Let us boast about nothing we've done,
God sacrificed His only beloved Son.

Put your hopes in a Mighty God.
True love that will not depart.

My God and Your God are the same,
He knows us all by our first name.

Paradise

God's in His heaven,

I am in my home.

He watches over me,

All the day long.

God knows my ending,

Before I begin.

He will protect me,

And keep me from sin.

God offers paradise,

I hunger to see.

He offers it to all,

And to all it is free.

Jesus is His Name

Jesus inspires me to live

He alone provides for my needs

Love is Jesus and Jesus is love

I look within myself to touch

His spirit that dwells within me

Peace and joy I have found

That which was always near by

He knows my limitations

Completed by His power and grace

I thank God for everything

A Speck of Dust

My God is all powerful,
His wisdom is beyond understanding.

God alone protects the world,
He gives it love, joy, peace, and hope.

He is the Creator of heavens and earth,
His name is above all names.

When I call on Him, he is there,
His presence removes all fears and doubts.

He knows me better than I know myself,
He soothes the mind and heart.

His Word offers eternal life,
Jesus is the way to salvation.

His love is for all human beings,
Even a speck of dust like me.

As His servant I never thirst or hunger,
He is the light of my life.

You Always Have a Plan

Through my darkest hour,
No matter how confused I was,
You always have a plan.

While I searched for answers,
No matter how alone I felt,
You always have a plan.

Deep down in my heart I knew,
No matter what shape the world is in,
You always have a plan.

I take this time to THANK YOU,
I am grateful that now I know,
That I am a part of that plan.

There is a Higher Order

There is a higher order,
That brings meaning to life.
It prepares the soul for heaven,
Offering what no man can promise.

There is a higher order,
It provides everlasting peace.
Mending the broken hearted,
Giving never ending love.

There is a higher order,
It tells of the Good News.
Cleansing even the filthy rages,
Showing charity for all.

There is a higher order,
Providing sight to the blind.
Filling the empty cup with oil,
Rescuing the down trodden.

There is a higher order,
That reaches high and low.
Touching the untouchables,
Washing them white as snow.

There is a higher order,
He is the King of Kings.
Offering everlasting life,
Rewarding His people.

Yes Lord!

This is the day the Lord has made;
let us rejoice and be glad in it.
Psalms 118:24

God Knows Your Heart

People judge by the clothes you wear,
They even judge by the color of your hair.
But God knows you by your heart,
He knew you from the start.

People judge by the things you own,
They desert you when your money is gone.
But God knows what you possess,
He offers you only the best.

People judge by the way you speak,
They help the rich and ignore the weak.
But God will supply all your needs,
He is the only way to succeed.

People judge you by where you live,
They like you for what you can give.
But God is the deliverer,
He is your Almighty Maker.

People judge by what they think you can do,
When you stop they turn their backs on you.
God gave you all of the talents you use,
He is the beginning of your good news.

People judge whether you are up or down,
They will step on you if you fall to the ground.
God created the heavens and the earth,
He is the only one that knows your worth.

People make promises that they cannot keep,
They will rob your dreams and steal your sleep.
God offers life and eternity,
He paved the way to set you free.

I Have Learned

I have learned to be patient,
I take one day at a time.
I learned how to find inner peace,
I keep a positive mind.

I have learned to use time wisely,
I treat each moment as my last.
I have learned not to worry about tomorrow,
I live in the present and not the past.

I have learned how to give and receive love,
I first had to love myself.
I have learned how to take care of me,
I am now able to take care of someone else.

I have learned to put God first,
I accept His will and not my own.
I have learned how to forgive myself,
I pick up the pieces and move on.

I have learned to discover the rainbows,
I believe God made them for me to see.
I have learned God loves us equally,
I know He wants us all to be free.

I have learned to have faith, trust and hope,
I know a man that has a plan.
I have learned where to take my problems,
I put them in Jesus' powerful hands.

Jesus I'm Ready to Listen

Precious Lord I am listening,
I hear and will do your command.

Yes, I will stop judging others,
I will work full time on myself.

Jesus, my eyes are open,
You have touched my heart.

You wake me up in the morning,
And I get up with joy from within.

Thank you for not giving up on me,
You renewed my strength so that I could live.

Joy rises in good times and bad because of you,
Your grace covers me like a blanket.

You gave me a new direction to follow,
I am grateful because you dwell wherever I go.

You have been like a cushion every time I fell,
You made even my rough roads seem smooth.

All my life I worried what others thought,
Now I focus and think for myself.

I realize that material gain is nothing,
My soul is the treasure that I must protect.

Life has found its meaning because of you,
I am able to fly like a bird and land safely.

My tears are wet and my pain hurts,
But because of You everything is alright.

I have found courage where once I had fear,
My heart sees your plan in all things.

Lord I Am Listening

I am listening to my happy heart,
It is telling me You will never part.

I am listening to Your Holy words,
They are the sweetest sounds, I ever heard.

I am listening to what the Bible says,
I will serve You all my days.

I am listening to Your Commandments,
I know that Your laws are heaven sent.

I am listening to Your love for me,
Lord, I love and believe in Thee.

I am listening to your amazing grace,
Your goodness can never be replaced.

I am listening to the joy You bring,
I praise Your Name through the songs I sing.

I am listening to equality of all men,
I love my brother because hate is sin.

I am listening to helping the poor,
Giving is receiving and I gained so much more.

I am listening to my need to pray,
I know you will show me the way.

Lord You Have Given Me Reasons

Lord, You have given me reasons for living,
You have given me reasons
for celebrating Thanksgiving.

Lord, You have given me reasons to carry on this fight,
You have given me reasons
to choose to do what is right.

Lord, You have given me reasons to pray each day,
You have given me reasons
to choose to do it your way.

Lord, You have given me reasons to know that I am loved,
You have given me reasons
to know it comes from heaven above.

Lord, You have given me reasons to sing and shout,
You have given me reasons
to know what living as a Christian is all about.

Lord, You have given me reasons to strive and to live,
You have given me reasons
to know how to forgive.

Lord, You have given me reasons to reach for the sky,
You have given me reasons
to let sin pass on by.

Lord, You have given me reasons to know You are Lord,
You have given me reasons
to climb on aboard.

Lord, You have given me reasons not to fuss and fight,
You have given me
knowledge and insight.

Lord, You have given me reasons to understand,
You have given me reasons
that help me to stand.

Lord, You have given me reasons to love and not to hate,
You have given me reasons
to change before it is too late.

Lord, You have given me reason when no one seems to care,
You have given me reasons
to know you will always be there.

Lord, You have given me reasons
to know you are good all the time,
You have given me reasons to find peace of mind.

Lord, You have given me reasons to wear a smile,
You have given me reasons
to be glad I am your child.

Lord, You have given me reasons to make me strong,
You have given me reasons
so I can go on.

Lord, You have given me reasons for me to believe,
You have given me reasons
to know that I can achieve.

Lord, You have given me reasons for divine healings,
You have given me reasons
for inspirational feelings.

Lord, You have given me reasons for me to give you my
heart, You have given me reasons,
for me having a brand new start.

Lord, You have given me reasons to sleep
peacefully at night, You have given me reasons,
to know everything will be all right.

Lord, You have given me reasons
to know that you are King of Kings,
You have given me reasons to put You above everything.

The Sun Will Still Shine

Your possessions that you leave behind
Will not bring you peace of mind

The willow tree still will sway
The sun will shine another day

Who will remember what you have done
Did you take time to help someone

Did your light glow for others to see
Were you the person that you wanted to be

The morning dew will still wet the ground
The world will still spin around

Did you love and do your best
Before you were laid to rest

A moment is all you have to give
It is not how long but how you live

Make no promises but do what you can
All of your tomorrows are in God's hands

Be Not Afraid

Though storms rage, be not afraid.

Though thunder crackle, be not afraid.

Though enemies plot, be not afraid.

Though troubles emerge, be not afraid.

Though friends desert, be not afraid.

Though loved ones pass on, be not afraid.

Though funds run low, be not afraid.

God loves you and will provide all.

If Time Could Stand Still

If time could stand still for that moment,
That feeling that rushed within.
That instant that life seemed so alive,
Filled with hope and promises to come.

If time could just stand still,
So that I could hold on to the moment,
When everything seem right and beautiful.
Peaceful and in touch with my soul.

If time could stand still for that moment,
That I knew what love felt like.
And I opened my heart and let it in,
I would rest on the shoulders of happiness.

If time could stand still for that moment,
That I know my Savior lives,
Giving me power within my spirit,
I know my strength comes from Him.

There is No Love
Like the Love of Jesus

There is no love like the love of Jesus,

One who died for me, so long ago at Calvary.

One who taught me how to live,

One who helps me to forgive.

One who sets my soul free,

One who loves me just for me.

He died and he suffered on the cross,

So that my soul would not be lost.

A love that lasts through eternity,

Thank you, Jesus for loving me.

Jesus Has Reached My Heart

I don't know much of anything,
But I do know that there is a God.

I know He loves and cares for me,
That puts joy into my living.

I have my good and bad days,
But, He offers me eternal peace.

I often make mistakes,
But he is a forgiving God.

I have been rejected and neglected,
He is always there to comfort me.

It took me awhile to find my way,
Now I know that Jesus is the way.

I use to live in fear and doubt,
But God has reached my heart.

I've Gotten My Joy
Back in My Heart

I've gotten my joy back in my heart,
Jehovah has given me a new start.

I've gotten my joy back in my soul,
God has truly made me whole.

I've gotten my joy back in my smile,
I'm so glad that I am His child.

I've gotten my joy back in my mind,
No better peace I will ever find.

I've gotten my joy back in my sight,
I know that my God will treat me right.

I've gotten my joy back into me,
Thank you God for setting me free.

What Do I Know?

I do not know what tomorrow may bring,

If I will be poor or have anything.

I do not know how long I will live,

If only this moment I have to give.

I do not know all of the answers why,

Good men have to suffer and they die.

But I am certain of this one thing,

My Lord and Savior is my King.

He has given me hope in a world corrupt,

He has forgiven my sins and cleaned me up.

I know that He lives inside me,

I have the faith that sets me free.

No problem is too big that He cannot solve,

Like salt in water it will dissolve.

He brings me joy in my darkest hour,

His mercy flows like April showers.

I'm Getting Ready to Live

I'm getting ready to live,
And it is all because of Him.

I'm laying down my old blues,
Putting on my running shoes.

I'm getting ready to live,
And it is all because of Him.

He gave me all my living tools,
Helped me with the Golden Rules.

I'm getting ready to live,
And it is all because of Him.

I've got no time to waste on sin,
He gave me what I need to win.

I'm getting ready to live,
I'm going to give all I have to give.

Running to the finish line,
Leaving all my foes behind.

I'm getting ready to live,
And it's all because of Him.

I'm going to nourish my soul,
With the One that made me whole.

I'm getting ready to live,
And it's all because of Him.

Letting Go

I Am,
Letting go of worldly things,
And the false sense that ownership brings.

I Am,
A part of the whole human race,
Not judging my brother by the color of his face.

I Am,
At rest with God,
Loving with my heart.

I Am,
Willing to change the way I think,
A power coming to life that will not sink.

I Am,
Forgiving myself and others too,
Saying goodbye to illusions that were not true.

I Am,
Feeling the presence for the very first time,
Embracing now and the peace that I find.

I Am,
Helping others wanting nothing in return,
Realizing this is something I had to learn.

I Am,
Aware of my presence and accept the here and now,
Releasing yesterday's burdens because today I know how.

My Soul Sings Victory

My faith remains steadfast,
I don't worry how long my troubles last.

I have inner peace from deep within,
My joy carries me through thick and thin.

I let go of problems and lean on the Lord,
His wisdom teaches me what to avoid.

I welcome my present the here and now,
My spirit has awaken and shown me how.

I have forgiven my worst enemy,
It gave freedom and set me free.

I am able to love with a clean heart,
It is love that keeps me closer to God.

I accept whatever my life brings,
I value people much more than things,

When I am still I feel divine,
My body is calm with a quiet mind.

I have stopped judging others,
I can see myself in my brothers.

My soul sings victory and is set to win.
I laid down my fear and let Jesus in.

Indescribable Music

The angels were singing
Sweet voices so gently bringing

Serene bliss to my soul
Drawn towards the melody

Surrendering all my heart
Accepting heaven on earth

Floating with joy into space
Drifting toward the light

Hearing the sounds from heaven
Filled with the Holy Spirit

Now I Feel It

Lord I listened to your Word,
I read the Bible to better understand.

I thought the verses in my mind,
I memorized them by heart.

I used your Word like a tool,
I quoted them to make my point.

I thought that I understood,
I took but did not receive.

My prayers were repetitious thoughts,
Often complaining and asking for more.

It wasn't until I put you in my heart,
That I could feel your Word.

My days and nights are all brand new,
I thank you for my life.

I hope and find joy in my soul,
And it is all because of you.

I feel your love that fills my world,
I surrender my soul to you.

I feel it, and now I know it,
Your Holy Spirit has awakened in me.

For the Love of God

For the love of God,
  I give my heart.

For the love of God,
  I will not part.

For the love of God,
  I know the way.

For the love of God,
  I hope and pray.

For the love of God,
  I am a friend.

For the love of God,
  I battle sin.

For the love of God,
  I will forgive.

For the love of God,
  I will live.

For the love of God,
  My soul is touched.

For the love of God,
My spirit is bold.

For the love of God,
I am humble and kind.

For the love of God,
I have peace of mind.

For the love of God,
I bear my pain.

For the love of God,
I have joy again.

For the love of God,
I understand.

For the love of God,
I am in His plan.

For the love of God,
I am born again.

For the love of God,
I will win.

Destiny

Lord, you control my destiny,
I know you work through me.

Lord you are my spirituality,
You have opened my heart to reality.

You always give me what I need,
By your grace I will succeed.

You gave me the strength to conquer all,
Good times or bad, I will stand tall.

You have removed my fear, pain and doubt,
Taught me what my purpose is about.

You erased my grief, anger and sorrow,
I cherish now, and won't worry about tomorrow.

I've forgiven my enemies and gotten rid of stress,
It's freed my soul and I've progressed.

It is all because of YOU,
That my life has become brand new.

Lord I Repent

Oh Lord, right now I repent,
I know your love is heaven sent.

I repent from all the lies I told,
My wicked ways that made me cold.

I repent from following the evil one,
I will stop taking credit for what you have done.

I repent from complaining the minute I arise,
I thank you Lord for opening my eyes.

I repent from gossiping about what others do,
I will try to help others or give it to you.

I repent from using your name in vain,
You answered my prayers over and over again.

I repent from not doing what you command,
I will put my heart and soul in Jesus' hand.

I repent from trying to defeat the devil alone,
I know when you are present the devil is gone.

Mary E. Darby

What Did I Learn From That

I've seen some storms in my life,
I lost my faith once or twice.

I've been miserable and all alone,
I had no place that I could call my own.

There was so much pain deep in my heart,
I thought my grief would tear me apart.

I've looked for someone to love me,
I thought I would lose my sanity.

I've talked but no one heard what I said,
Confusing thoughts seemed to fill my head.

I've longed just to be understood,
I wondered who would help me if they could.

I've watched my dreams go up in smoke,
My money went and I was broke.

I've searched for friends that I could call,
But I could not find anyone at all.

My bills were up and my funds were low,
I listened to others tell me they told me so.

Somewhere in the midst of my soul,
I asked the question that made me whole.

What did I learn from my discord in life,
Did I learn how to carry on through strife?

I sought deep within to bring out my best,
I viewed my hard times as only a test.

I fought to keep my apparitions alive,
It is when times are rough that I must strive.

What did I learn from all the problems I had,
That God will get me through the good times and bad.

I Sing a Song

I sing the song
I know the words
The sweetest verse
I ever heard
Yes, Jesus loves me
Yes, Jesus loves me

I feel His love
I know His power
He leads me
Through my darkest hour
Yes, Jesus guides me
Yes, Jesus guides me

I witness His wonders
I know that He lives
He is in my heart
Eternal life He gives
Yes, Jesus saved me
Yes, Jesus saved me

The Joy of Loving God

The joy of loving God,
It is complete fulfillment.

The peace in knowing God,
Calms your soul and frees your mind.

The faith of believing in God,
Gives hope to survive each day.

The power of depending on God,
It strengthens your heart and inner spirit.

The wisdom that comes from God,
It gives knowledge to make good decisions.

The love of accepting God,
It completes all understanding of life.

I Have It All

What I have as I carry on,
It cannot be seen by eyes alone.

It gives me strength when it appears,
It brings me hope and calms my fears.

It carries me when I can no longer walk,
It speaks for me when I cannot talk.

My thoughts are dreams I know will come true,
I believe that God will carry me through.

I know that all things work as they should,
My Father knows what's best for my good.

I have faith I'm connected to a higher power,
It washes me clean like an April shower.

I am able to feel the wonder of His love,
It touches my heart from heaven above.

No, I do not deserve this gift of life,
My Jesus died and paid the price.

I sometimes stumble but do not fall,
He always hears my plea when I call.

How sweet it is to know the King.
How sweet to know the joy it brings.

He opened my eyes so I could see,
It's His deliverance that set me free.

I pray that my soul is His to keep,
I know He will awake me when I sleep.

Lord I Am Coming Home

Lord, I am coming home,
I've been lost in this world too long.

I've been wandering around,
I've been feeling empty and beat down.

Lord, I m seeking your love,
Let it rain from heaven above.

I've been searching but I could not fine,
I could not get any peace of mine.

Lord, I recognize that it is true,
I am less than nothing without you.

I thought I knew it all,
But my conceit caused me to fall.

Lord, I am seeking your grace,
I believe you have prepared me a place.

I was lost now but now I am able to see,
I have faith that you will save me.

Lord, I am calling out your name,
I know my cry will not be in vain.

I realize everything you offer is free,
I am thankful that you hear my plea.

Lord, I am offering you my heart,
I kneel down to you for a new start.

Life Down Here

If God is for us, who is against us?
Romans 8:31

I Wear a Mask

I wear a mask,
It covers my face, it hides my feelings,
So no one sees,
My struggle that goes on inside of me.

I wear a mask,
To shield my fear, I look real bold,
My appearance is strong,
It makes me look like nothing is wrong.

I wear a mask,
When I am blue, it shelters my sadness,
My tears are dry,
I laugh out loud, when I want to cry.

I wear a mask,
It feeds my pride, it gives me false confidence,
My self esteem is very low,
I hurt inside but it does not show.

I wear a mask,
It conceals my pain, my heart seeks love,
But my persona says no,
My isolation asserts that I desire it so.

I wear a mask,
When I think all hope is gone,
I fall to my knees and bow my head.
My eyes are closed but my soul can see,

That my God knows what's inside of me.

So Tired of Being Tired

Tired of being timid and alone,
Tired of wishing my troubles were gone.

Tired of worrying about what others say,
Tired of letting people stand in my way.

Tired of thinking negative ideas that keep me down,
Tired of acting a fool and being a clown.

Tired of being helpless with nothing to give,
Tired of feeling sorry for myself and how I live.

Tired of giving permission for others to use me,
Tired of making the same mistakes because I cannot see.

Tired of minding others' business instead of mine,
Tired of playing a role and pretending that I'm fine.

Tired of trying to please everyone when I am sad,
Tired of searching for true love that I never had.

Tired deep down in my soul of facing all my fears,
Tired of being, tired of being, tired for all these years.

Who Am I?

I am not the names they call me,
Though I perform many roles.

What I look like on the outside,
Cannot define my soul.

My past has gone and left me,
I must leave it behind.

My present is all I have right now,
I embrace it because it is mine.

I cannot wait for tomorrow,
It steals my time away.

I am alive this moment,
I feel the joy of living today.

Birds flying high in the trees,
Singing as they go.

What peace I find in the stillness,
To understand that God loves me so.

I Am Working on the Building

I am working on my building,
Pain doesn't live here anymore.

I have laid my foundation,
I know what I'm living for.

I have the only contractor,
That can build me a home.

I have faith I'll have my mansion,
And it won't be long.

I'm going to open up my windows,
And let the fresh air in.

I'm going to clean out my closets,
And I'm throwing away sin.

I am working on my building,
Jesus gave me the tools.

He gave me all the materials,
That I will ever need to use.

Take Time to Live

Now is the moment, to take time to live,
Stop doing just what appears good.

Putting on a show for others to see,
This is the time to do what you should.

Busy working to acquire more things,
You're too tired to remember the reasons why.

You've lost touch with family and friends,
And life has no meaning as it slips by.

Guilt fills your mind when you relax and rest,
You feel emptiness inside that you cannot explain.

Some people have taken you for granted,
Self doubt has caused you much pain.

Now is the time to regain your hope and faith,
Listen to your heartbeat and find what's inside.

Let go of fake ego, it's destroying who you are,
Your self-esteem doesn't need false pride.

Give yourself permission to love from deep within,
Your soul is connected to the highest power.

Joy springs from your spirit even when you're down,
Take a deep breath and be alive this hour.

Your aspirations are not in vain,
Know there's one that makes everything possible.

Be patient and wait on the Lord that cares,
He is the master over all things impossible.

Now is the time for you to live,
And discover the joy of living.

Put down your heavy burdens,
And live the life you have been given.

Thank You Has Many Meanings

Thank you has many meanings,
It signifies you are appreciated.

You were thoughtful and considerate,
Your act improved someone's situation.

You took the time to do something kind,
Your labor benefited another person.

You gave yourself unselfishly,
Your support gave joy to someone else.

You said something nice to a person,
Your comments were received favorably.

You wore a smile that reflected friendliness,
Your beam was received with a grin.

You shared your wealth with others,
Your charity returned rays of sunshine to you.

You accepted thank you and you're welcome,
Your spirit radiates the compassionate
and loving being you are.

Thank You!

Lost and Found

Have you ever been lost
standing on old familiar ground

Were you surrounded by people
but no one could be found

Could your mind recall
memories present or the past

Did you wonder what was happening
but you were too afraid to ask

When you woke up this morning
were you in your right mind

Did ideas that once came quickly
you just could not seem to find

Did your dreams hit a ceiling
they stopped climbing up the hill

Once you were young and hopeful
now, you are standing still

Were you living in the moment
but things were not so clear

Did you ask yourself the question
like, why am I here

Were you able to find the answers
that comes from deep inside

Did you know that Jesus loves you
that He never leaves your side

My Ego

My ego loves to chatter,
It tells me what to do.

It tears down my self-image.
It makes me feel blue.

If my outlook is optimistic,
It will find something negative to say.

It takes my sense of humor,
And turns it the other way.

It described my self-esteem,
Said it was nothing but titles and roles.

It hindered my self-confidence,
And put down all my goals.

It encouraged me to lose my temper,
Say whatever I thought.

I never once heard it tell me,
I should choose the battles I fought.

Now I see its many faces,
How it has led me astray.

The next time I see ego,
I will quietly slip away.

The Paths We Take

Life is filled with choices,
They determine the road you take.

Sometimes they can be easy,
Often they are difficult to make.

When they run in two directions,
One is all you can pick.

At times, what you choose does not matter,
The outcome will still make you sick.

The powerful rule over decisions,
Implanting seeds of dignity or servitude.

Supremacy writes its own values,
Defining who is civilized or crude.

Even a caged bird has options,
It can opt to sing or not.

Some people choose to be unhappy,
No matter how much they have got.

A number of people find joy,
They decide to look inside.

A choice to discover one's self,
Walks out on ego and pride.

What Will Make Me Worthy?

How can I become acceptable
to kneel before the King?

What must I have,
and what should I bring?

When do I start preparing,
to go before His throne?

Will I have enough time,
to correct what I've done wrong?

What will be my answer,
when He asks me what I've done?

Can I truly answer,
Lord, I made you Number One.

Where can I go,
to find what I need?

Who can instruct me,
so that I will succeed?

Why does He love someone,
as ordinary as me?

Have I done all I should,
to make myself worthy?

A House is Not a Home

A house is shelter to reside,
A home is love that you feel inside.

A house is a location to dwell,
A home is the feeling that all is well.

A house is the space filled with things,
A home is the satisfaction it brings.

A house is the price that it is worth,
Home is the blessings on this earth.

A house is a residence to live,
A home is the peace of mind that it gives.

A house is a roof over your head,
A home is the place where you get fed.

A house is a construction with walls,
A home is a safety net when you fall.

A house is a building made of stone or wood,
A home is the soul of feeling good.

I Must Look Inside

My battle is not yours, my friend,
The battle I fight is deep within.

I must look inside of me,
I seek to find self-discovery.

There are so many parts of me to know,
So many parts to find and me to show.

There is a part that is still a child,
I will hug, kiss, and give a smile.

There is a part of me that is called my past,
I will use what I learned to make it last.

I will see things I don't want to see,
Facing these things will set me free.

My good memories I will use to build,
I will take one step at a time as I journey uphill.

I must look inside of me to find,
That wonderful thing called peace of mind.

Who can study me better than I myself?
I know me better than anyone else.

So Much Pain Over Foolishness

So much pain over foolishness,
Doing things we will regret.

If we love God, we love our brother,
We would stop the hate and killing each other.

Desiring material things and selling our souls,
Betraying others while our hearts grow cold.

Came in this world naked and bare,
Death won't let us take anything, anywhere.

Using cruel words and calling them jokes,
Is just a cover up to tear down folks.

Families become strangers when they put up walls,
The higher they go, the harder they will fall.

Nobody is perfect, we must strive to do well,
Only Jesus is perfect, and can keep us from hell.

Envy and greed is the devil's best tools,
He has skillfully used them to change us to fools.

Our mistakes have lessons to aid us to grow,
They reveal something that we should know.

We must be humble, we have nothing to boast,
Comparing who has the least or who has the most.

The answers we seek come from God,
We judge appearances but He knows our hearts.

The people we have hurt doesn't lead to success,
Making people feel good gives us more not less.

We are always trying to show we are smart,
If we want true wisdom, we can find it through God.

Living

I will dream while I sleep,

When I awaken I will live my life.

I will not regret what I did or did not do,

I will be too busy doing what I can do.

Tomorrow May Never Come

This is the first day of my life.

This is the middle of my life.

This is the worst day of my life.

This is the best day of my life.

This is the saddest day of my life.

This is the happiest day of my life.

This is the slowest day of my life.

This is the fastest day of my life.

This is the coolest day of my life.

This is hottest day of my life.

This is the dumbest day of my life.

This is the smartest day of my life.

This is the hardest day of my life.

This is the last day of my life,

Because tomorrow may never come.

The Greatness in You

I can see the greatness inside of you,
Success destined to come through.

Think about what you want to achieve,
Life will attract whatever you conceive.

Dream big, and focus on your quest,
Life in return will always give you the best.

Magnetize love, peace and hope in your mind.
Think about the joy that your heart wants to find.

Realize that trouble is just a part of life,
Accept what is, and release anger and strife.

Believe you are a winner and it will come true.
God has provided the greatness inside of you.

Joy

I stood and watched a rainbow,
The sun was shining bright.

I felt a sense of peace surround me,
I knew everything would be alright.

I heard some birds sweetly chirping,
I watched as they flew swiftly by.

Tears of joy wet my face,
As I gently began to cry.

I Can

I Can,
Fight for the things that I believe,
Do my best so that I will succeed.

I Can,
Respect my brother regardless of his race,
Judge not the color of his face.

I Can,
Believe in God and keep my faith,
Know that He is the keeper of my fate.

I Can,
Love myself the way that I am,
Be as strong as a lion or gentle as a lamb.

I Can,
Forgive myself and others too,
Free myself from feeling blue.

I Can,
Fail at some things and continue on,
Keep hope alive until my doubts are gone.

I Can,
Help somebody wanting nothing in return,
Seek an education because I want to learn.

I Can,
Change my world by the way I think,
Hold on to my dreams so that they will not sink.

The Inner Self

The inner self is inside of me,
Now is always present.

The past has already happened,
My time is this moment.

Love is that divine connection,
It touches the God in me.

Life has a beginning and end,
I will accept the time in between.

Forgiveness liberates the body pain,
It gives peace to my soul.

What Does it Look Like?

What does it look like, asked Ego,
Is it as great as I am?

It's not half as beautiful as me,
Answered, Boastful,

Doesn't belong with my kind,
Shouted, Prejudice.

I bet I could do much better than it,
Wagered, Competition.

I can just look at it and tell I can't stand it,
Raged, Hatred.

I don't judge by outward appearance,
Stated, Harmony.

I can see myself in it,
Said, Love,

It looks like a chance to make a friend,
Cheered, Peaceful.

Let us unite and be as one,
Encouraged, Unity.

Peace is Better

Even when I think I am right,
Making peace is better.

Even when I can win an argument,
I know that peace is better.

Even when I want to have the last word,
I am silent because peace is better.

Even when I let go of anger and ego,
I release both because peace is better.

Even if I disagree with my brother,
I find a common ground because peace is better.

Even as I strive along my journey,
I know that peace makes it better.

I'm Only Human

I am only human,
Filled with my mistakes.

I can only tell you,
I do not always have what it takes.

If I offend you,
Please try to understand.

I am trying to do my best,
At least that is my plan.

It's too hard to please,
And do what everyone else thinks.

I've got to trust my feelings,
Whether I stand or sink.

God alone will judge me,
I am trying to do His will.

Imperfections never leave me,
But I know that my faith is real.

I must search my heart and soul,
Within my spirit strives for love.

I must give it on earth,
In order to receive from up above.

Daily I pray for forgiveness,
And my burdens I will bear.

I give my all to Jesus,
I believe His justice is fair.

With a Word

With a word, I can be polite,
Or act very rude.

I can choose to be kind,
Or show an insensitive mood.

I can reveal love,
Or demonstrate hate.

I can decide to ask forgiveness,
Or make vengeance my fate.

I can be supportive,
Or destroy someone's quietness.

I can give a compliment,
Or make someone else feel less.

I can say hello,
Or turn my face not to speak.

I can show how strong my faith is,
Or reveal that it is weak.

I can spread good news,
Or gossip and put others down.

I can be constructive,
Or knock someone to the ground.

I can give God praises,
Or show my evil side.

I can be humble,
Or be guided by pride.

I can offer compassion,
Or I can show no empathy,

I can accept others,
Or act like the world turns only for me.

I can make a friend,
Or create an enemy.

Just with a word, I can make a difference,
And it is all up to me.

Right Now I Am Alive

Right here, right now I am alive,
Let me use my time being grateful.

Many family and friends passed away,
Let their lives give me strength to go on.

How precious is this hour that I won't waste,
Even a moment on envy, hatred or deceit.

I will shout with praise all the day long,
Giving thanks to God for touching my soul.

Right here, right now I am alive,
This gift I will cherish and love.

I will dance to the beat of my heart,
Because I know the God that I serve.

I have peace within that reaches the sky,
And hope, faith, and grace that set me free.

I am grateful that I accepted Jesus,
He is the light that makes my light shine.

Right here, right, now, I am alive,
My spirit soars to the heavens.

I'm Telling You

I'm telling you to pray right,
I'm telling you to stay right.

I'm telling you to see right,
I'm telling you to be right.

I'm telling you to go right,
I'm telling you to know right.

I'm telling you to walk right,
I'm telling you to talk right.

I'm telling you to live right,
I'm telling you to forgive right.

I'm telling you to plan right,
I'm telling you to stand right.

I'm telling you to do right,
I'm telling you to pursue right.

I'm telling you to receive right,
I'm telling you to believe right.

From This Moment On

From this moment on,
I promise to always love you.

I will not look backward at the past,
I will not worry about what did not last.

Imprisoned by the love I once had,
I am free whether it was good or bad.

From this moment on,
I promise to make joy my song.

I will cherish the feelings that I feel,
You make me happy and that is real.

From this moment on,
I will not blame others for what went wrong.

I will use my powers to reach for success,
I will use my thoughts for what I do best.

From this moment on,
I will not feel alone.

My inner peace caresses my soul,
I have something more precious than gold.

From this moment on,
I will have protection through the storm.

You will drive away all of my fears,
I will gently wipe away all of my tears.

From this moment on,
I will change win, to won.

I will be there for me,
I will look inside, and realize it is already done.

The Journey

I am going to enjoy my life journey,
I will be thankful for every moment now.

I won't lean on my own understanding,
I will ask God to show me how.

I am letting go of complaining,
I will just do what I can.

If I stumble and fall down,
I will simply get up and stand.

I will stop trying to fix others behavior,
Then I can work on me doing right.

I must strive and protect my own soul,
This is a battle, I have to fight.

I am going to embrace the bad times,
I have my faith to carry me through.

I am going to look for the joy in life,
And do my best in everything I do.

I Am Finally Free

Like the river flowing into the ocean,
I feel my spirit awakening to love.

Like the sunrise that lights the earth,
My heart is beating with joy.

Like a new born baby entering the world,
I see God's wonders all around me.

Like the birds that fly high and sing,
My life is a song called thankful.

Like rain drops on dry soil,
I am finally free.

Life is Simple

Life is so simple,
It offers many opportunities for hope.

Everyone receives exactly what they want,
There are no big I's and little you's.

If you believe it is a good day,
Then you will climb every mountain.

If you believe you are bored,
Then nothing exciting will enter your world.

Stand still and just listen to the sounds of life,
You might hear your heart beating like drums.

No one escapes untouched by problems,
They provide lessons to survive.

People that respect and love other people,
They walk in the Garden of Eden.

Now is all the time you can count on,
Find the joy of the moment.

Naked you entered the world,
What will you take when you leave?

Whatever you give freely to help others,
It returns tenfold to enrich your spirit.

Accepting the differences in others,
It frees your inner self.

All life is connected,
Your thoughts and actions do matter.

Be thankful in good and bad times,
Eventually, this too will pass.

About the Author

Mary E. Darby was born in Chester, South Carolina, the eldest of nine children. She grew up in Washington D.C. and moved to Los Angeles, California as a young adult. For more than 30 years, Mary taught elementary school while raising her two daughters, Sylvia and Nicole and grandson, Brandon.

In May 2011, Mary was diagnosed with a rare condition and had major spinal surgery. After complications and two additional surgeries in less than two months, she was paralyzed. Mary was in and out of the hospital for five months and she spent 13 consecutive weeks in a critical care unit and at a rehabilitation center. Mary has learned to walk again and is getting stronger every day.

Mary has been writing poetry as long as she can remember. Her poetic motivation is to express her emotions and to inspire others through the journey of life. Mary's work touches a universal cord due to her depth of faith and real understanding of the human condition. *Living by Faith* is her first book of poetry.

www.ingramcontent.com/pod-product-compliance
Lightning Source LLC
LaVergne TN
LVHW051641080426
835511LV00016B/2423